JOURNEY TO PURPOSE

My life of purpose

BY

Nordine Campbell

Copyright © 2015 **Nordine Campbell**

Published by Agape Behaviour publishing

All rights reserved

Unless otherwise indicated, all Scripture quotations are from The Holy Bible, NKJV, New King James Version

Contents

Introduction 1
Appreciation 2
About the Author 3
Foreword 5

Chapter 1. Was it a curse? 7
Chapter 2. Family and Church 11
Chapter 3. Life Changed 19
Chapter 4. Abuse at 'The Park' 23
Chapter 5. Homeless 30
Chapter 6. Education 42
Chapter 7. Reconciliation 57

Journey to Purpose notes 63

INTRODUCTION

Journey to Purpose

As I have struggled with infertility and subsequently had a hysterectomy (removing of the womb) at the age of 25, barrenness or infertility, is a topic that has, for obvious reasons, interested me since I know that many women face this issue and are living in shame, secrecy and depression.

The summary of the benefits and curses of the law as given to Moses by God shows that if the nation were to be obedient there would not be any barren men, women or animals in their population. It also shows that God himself is capable of either shutting up a womb or opening it as he wishes. Exodus 23:26, Deuteronomy 7:14.

As I try to share my story of challenges, fears and victories, I hope it will be a blessing to all who read it.

Nordine Campbell

Appreciation

My special thanks to the Holy Spirit for inspiring me to write this book, *Journey to Purpose*.

My sincere appreciation to my long-standing friend Paul Clifford for his long suffering, for listening to me and encouraging me to pursue my ambition to return to school and pushing me even when I wanted to give up.

My thanks to Irene, my sister and best friend, for following me everywhere I moved to and being there for me through sickness, health and for maintaining the family connection.

Dr Mohammed Johnson, I appreciate your encouragement and for challenging me to write this book. I was so excited to see this book come to life after spending 5 years on my computer.

And finally, I am grateful to both my father and mother for shaping my life.

R.I.P. my sister, Pauline. You are never forgotten.

About the Author

Pastor Nordine Campbell is the CEO/founder of **Centre of Hope** Global Ministries and Children's Charity that operates internationally. She is also a Reverend Minister, philanthropist, educationalist, professional life coach, international preacher and an apostle.

Her international operations include work in the UK, Ghana, Uganda, Kenya and Jamaica. Through her organisation **Centre of Hope**, her main objective is to promote charitable purposes, for the benefit of children living in the UK and developing countries and in particular to relieve poverty and sickness, advance the education and protect the good health of children.

Centre of Hope were recipients of the following awards: Excellence For Educational Services Award 2004, UK; Children's Educational Charity of the year Award, 2004, UK; and Excellent Mama Africa Award, Ghana, 2012.

She is a dynamic leader, teacher and speaker as well as being a mother and mentor to many.

Foreword

'Woman of God Apostle Nordine Campbell is a great woman with a spirit of faith driven by her compassion for mankind. My encounter with her became the turning point of my life and the highest honour from me was to name my son after her dad and my daughter after her.

The book *Journey To Purpose* is indeed a classic piece. You just can't resist but to be imparted.'

**Proud son, Jude Brapah – Founder/CEO,
Brapah World Life Coaching & Outreach, Ghana.**

'This is a graphical presentation of the author's life. Today, we fondly remember how our godlike mother trained us to live our lives in conformity to both divine and societal expectation. We owe our success to her defined leadership in our home. The book will provoke you to achieve the best on this journey of unravelling the secret of a purposeful life'.

**Bob and Martha Hemans,
Holy Child School Cape Coast, Ghana.**

'In the *Journey To Purpose*, the author Rev. Nordine Campbell shares with the reader her explicit life time experience which I strongly recommend for every Leader,

Pastor, Entrepreneur or any Leader in any capacity who has received a specific mandate to accomplish a purpose.'

Maxwell Osei Okley – Pastor,
Centre of Hope Global Ministry, Ghana.

'A woman of God attested with living testimonies of God's mercy, love and protection. Her life's story as a Pastor's daughter who struggled and overcame, can change your destiny, identity and catapult you to the next level in life. Her new book *Journey to Purpose* unfolds mysteries in life. It is a masterpiece of revelations and insights which brings illumination of encouragement and faith in God. I encourage you to have a copy and read through its pages prayerfully.'

Bishop Dr Samuel Yankyerah – Africa,
Director for Pentecostal International.

CHAPTER 1

Was it a curse?

I became curious as to what the Bible had to say about infertility. I was surprised at what I discovered. I have no statistics concerning the rate of infertility, but I suppose it was higher since there were no tests, procedures, or fertility drugs available back then, (I do know that mother and infant mortality were higher due to lack of medical care).

Children were a sign of God's blessing, so all couples dreaded infertility. It was a stigma not to have children. What had a person done wrong to incur the punishment of God? The question that arose many times in my mind and prayers during the tearful nights was as follows: **Are barren or childless women cursed?**

From a quick search, I discovered in the Bible that there were *seven* women who were initially barren, but six of them did finally conceive after many years. In those days it was a shame for a woman not to bear her husband's children, but they did not always understand as we do today, that sometimes it is the *'husband'* who is infertile rather than the wife.

This matter is personal as I have had no children and been living like this. When I first realised that I would never conceive it was a shock to me and it gave me so much pain. Some people, especially men, do not see childlessness as a positive even if they have had their own. They see you as a freak that would not be fulfilled.

I know that there are many women who are living with childlessness and are suffering in silence. Many of these married women are feeling embarrassed when asked about their children.

Women have experienced divorce due to childlessness and some women never married because they felt they would never be accepted as a good enough wife.

In some cultures men take a second wife. In the Bible, Elkanah took a second wife Peninnah because his first and favourite wife Hannah could not bear children.

See **Samuel chapter 1, chapter 2 verses 1-21.**

This special woman Hannah, meaning *'gracious'* or *'favour'*, was unable to conceive. I am sure she did not feel gracious or highly favoured due to this. Like Hannah, many women have gone through the pain of ridicule and taunting from other women and their in-laws.

The Bible says that children are a blessing and children are our heritage; therefore, women without children believe that they must be cursed if they are unable to produce that blessing and obtain the inheritance by having children. Every woman has her story and some of them are horrendous, so bad that they are too ashamed to tell their stories.

My stories begin when I was fourteen years old. I was gang raped. The drama that followed was more hurtful than the actual rape, as gruesome as it was.

As a 'PK' *(Pastor's Kid*/daughter), the first born child, and the first born daughter out of ten children you could imagine the expectations of many including my father and mother. My father was not any ordinary pastor but the founder of the First Black-led church in our town.

For the first time, I saw my father in a place where he did not know what to do. Several meetings followed. In the meantime I was dragged from one hospital department to another going through numerous tests, for what? I cannot even remember as it was so overwhelming to me, I remember just wanting to die, because I found myself in a place where I did not want to be.

I spent sleepless nights worrying about what would happen to me. My father was very angry not only that his daughter was subjected to this horrific act, but that his reputation as a pastor and a upstanding man in the community could be experiencing such disgrace.

To top it all, one of the boys that had raped me was a son of one of his congregation members. I went through so much condemnation and guilt. I condemned myself because I thought maybe I had done something that caused this to happen, even though I knew that was not true.

I just had to try to make sense of it all. How was my father dealing with this matter? At the time I felt that my father was not dealing with this situation in the best way; I needed someone to tell me it was all going to be ok. Instead, my siblings were told not to talk to me and I was scorned.

If I was in the kitchen when my mum was making a cup of tea for my father, he would refuse it. I was made to sleep on a sun lounger in the bedroom as my sisters shared a room. I was not allowed to go and sleep in the same bed as my sister, and she was warned that if she allowed me to sleep in her bed she would be beaten. On occasions during the night, my father would come and check that I was not sharing the bed with my sister.

I dreaded what my father would do to me. He did not say anything or really talk about things. I was truly convinced that he would put me in a home or banish me for my sins and most of all for bringing shame into his house and on his precious church people; he spent most of his time going from house to house praying for them as if the prayers they received in church were not enough.

CHAPTER 2

Family and Church

I was born in Jamaica in a place called Endeavour, Manchester, in 1957, to a deacon and sister Campbell. Being the first born I know that my father and mother were looking forward to the day of my birth with prayer. My mother had a good pregnancy when she was carrying me in the comfort of her womb.

My mother explained that preparation began for my arrival. Then one night my mum had a dream. In her dream she saw two black dogs and they licked the palm of her hands. She awoke in panic, found she was dumb and could not speak for two weeks.

The church my parents attended called a fast. Day and night they fasted and prayed and had all night vigils, praying for a safe birth and that mother and child would pull through. Then one day there was a breakthrough, my mother uttered her first word, "Hallelujah", and went immediately into labour. It took two days of walking up and down before I came into this world, by God's grace and prayer.

One year later, my sister Irene was born. A few years later, my parents experienced a troublesome fate; their home was engulfed in fire and they lost everything. Soon after, my father was invited to England for a better life by his brother who was already in England. My father took up the invitation and left my mother with two young children. My mother followed him once my sister was weaned, and left us with our grandmother, Maud Stevenson. We joined them later when I was 6 years old and my sister Irene was 5.

I remember I had a great bond with my grandmother and was not happy to leave her, even though she prepared us to reunite with our parents with pictures of snow and how nice it would be in England. As far as I was concerned these people were strangers and my grandmother was my mum. She was all I knew and of course, my sister and I did not want to leave her behind, we wanted to stay with her.

I remember crying and protesting. It took me a long time to accept my father as my father and I don't think that we had bonded very well from the beginning.

I was a child that spoke my mind and my father thought I was too forward with my opinions, even as young as I was.

I found it very hard to settle down at school and had many run-ins with the teachers. Most of the time the teachers complained; they did not understand what I was saying and thought that I was too cheeky.

My father found it very difficult to deal with this so his way was to punish me by beating me and threatening to send me back home. What he did not know was that his threats gave me an incentive, as it was just what I wanted, 'to go back home'.

I was expected to be grown up and take responsibility for my siblings when we arrived in the UK. We came and met 3 other children Robert, Stephen and Grace.

My mother had another child shortly after we arrived. I remember there was an explosion in the kitchen; someone had left the gas oven on and when my mum went to light it, it exploded while she was pregnant. She was rush to hospital where she had the baby. He was called Gilbert. One year later she had my sister, Pauline, who died at 6 months old from cot death.

There was a feeling that we were sent to the UK to help my mother look after the small ones. I don't know how my sister Irene felt, but I felt I did not fit into this family and I often dreamt of going back in my early years.

When I did not do my homework or I came in tired to school because we were at church till late, my excuse was always that I had to look after my brothers and sisters.

My mum would go mad when the school would call and tell her what I said. Even now my siblings jest, "You lot came here to look after us", (meaning my sister and me). It was not easy living here as there was a lot of racism at the time.

Luton was a developing town with lots of factories, so people came to Luton for work. Vauxhall, Electrolux and a new airport were the major employers and of course many hat factories, which was the main industry in Luton. The first feature of Luton was in *Alice in Wonderland*; the mad hatter came from Luton.

Before the black people came to Luton the Irish were the first immigrants, but many of them went mad because of the mercury that they used to soften the felt that made the hats. It would get into their skin and noses from the smell and caused brain damage. When realising this, they stopped making felt hats and made more straw hats.

When my father came to Luton, there was still signs in shop windows and doors that said: **No Irish, No Niggers and No dogs.**

My Father: Pastor Egbert Campbell. Born in Jamaica to a farmer, he was the first of three sons. His second brother was called Carlton, and there was a younger brother who was disabled. There was not a lot said about him, therefore I am not aware of his name.

My father died of a massive stroke in 1996; from the day of the stroke he spoke not a word until his death, 6 days later.

He was a very strict dad and loved his children, worked hard as a pastor and during the day as a paint worker in Electrolux.

As children we looked forward to him coming home, see who would be the first to meet him coming down the road to receive him and collect his work bag. Whoever got there first would receive the gift inside the bag, (I don't think he could afford to bring presents for all of us as at that time there were eight children in the house).

He was a good provider and we never gone without. My mum told me that Electrolux had a strike. My father applied for benefit to tide him over during the strike and the benefit office sent him £1 to feed 8 children, his wife and himself. He framed the cheque of the £1 they offered him.

Mum said he would go to work without having breakfast, he had no dinner until he came home and sometimes there would not be enough food for us and my parents. They would often go to bed hungry praying for a breakthrough, just to make sure we could eat.

My mum told me that when we were at school, she would pray because often there would not be anything for us to eat when we came home.

One day she was praying and she heard a voice say, "Put the pot on with some water." She got up from her knees and did as she was instructed. By the time the water began to boil, there was a knock at the front door. Someone had come with a box of provisions sent with a driver. To this day, she never knew who sent them.

In the box was everything she needed for the rest of the week and more, just as Paul said to the Philippians: 4:19 in the Bible: "And God shall supply all your needs according to His riches in Glory."

Throughout their lives many, many miracles happened, and their church grew.

One day came a bombshell. A spirit had entered the church in the form of a bishop. The head office in America sent a bishop over to oversee the church in England as it had grown more than they had anticipated.

We would see hundreds of people come for our annual conventions. We had to rent the biggest venue we could find to host it.

We, the children, enjoyed it; we could show off our talent, meet new people from other churches from all over the world including England. When they had their conventions we would reciprocate, but often my mum was not able to go because she had too many children and there was often no room for all of us and others in the church minibus.

It turned out that the bishop, who is dead now (only death could stop him), was a paedophile. They had got rid of him by sending him to us without the knowledge of my father.

It wasn't until mothers started to bring their pregnant daughters to my dad accusing the bishop as the culprit (accusations which turned to be true), that he was discovered. There were four girls and others who came out of the woodwork of molestation.

He had access because he worked full-time in the church and did all the administration. Children that were not at school for whatever reason would be sent to the church to help out in the office, to do their homework until their parents finished work, or on a Saturday after doing our own housework, would be sent to the church to clean it and help to get it ready for the Sunday service.

He would be in the office and would call his favourite to come and help him sort the office out and would reward them with sweets or a gift.

Unfortunately one Saturday morning I was there on my own, as the other girls had not yet arrived and he came in. I must add that I was not one of his favourites because I was too cheeky and answered back. He called me to his office, I came to the door and he exposed himself to me. He told me to come in but I refused.

He got up and grabbed my arm. I pulled myself away and said, "If you touch me, I'm going to tell my dad." He said, "He won't believe you." I ran away because I felt very uncomfortable. I would never go there on my own again unless someone was with me.

I was scared to tell in case I got into trouble. He disappeared and never came back after being confronted regarding the pregnant girls.

He was not the only culprit. There were others in the church that groomed young girls and boys, some of whom are still alive, go to church and hold positions of trust.

All I knew was that my dad was in a lot of trouble because he left the church in a financial mess. Eventually the church was closed and we had to move; it was the summer of 1970. My dad left the COGIC church and joined The Firstborn Church.

CHAPTER 3

Life Changed

I remember because it was just after our summer holiday, and when we returned to school the evenings were always bright.

I loved landscaped gardens, so after school I would take the long way around feasting my eyes, wishing and dreaming that when I got older I would buy one of those big houses. I dreamt that I would have my own room instead of sharing with my sisters, I would dream of having abeautiful well-kept garden, with my own gardener.

By the time I got home, the time had gone and I would be late. Now, this was a problem for my mum as she would be worried about me and as I was the eldest of nine children, she depended on me to relieve her of some of the duties she had to perform such as preparing dinner, getting the other children changed and setting the house in order for when my father got home.

Imagine me telling her that I was on my own, sightseeing. "Sightseeing?" Slap! "When there is so much to do? Stop lying, you was out with your friends." "No mammy, I was out by myself."

I did not know how it sounded at the time, but this would happen every day and I now know why I did it.

Our house was overcrowded; there was never a place in our house to breathe. So this was my only opportunity to be on my own before going home. My mother would always threaten to tell my father, but I could not stop it.

This was my freedom, my space; I needed to get prepared to face all the children, do the chores and attend prayer meetings in the house, plus I was still getting used to being here. I came from Jamaica when I was 6 years old; I came in October 1963, the coldest winter ever, could you imagine? Even at 14 years old I was still missing my grandmother and some of the life I had in Jamaica.

On one evening after school I met Mrs Althorn (not her real name) on the way home.

She was burdened down with bags. She used to live at our house until her son came over from Jamaica. My parents always rented a room in our house to help with the bills or to help those that came into the country until they found somewhere to live.

As I got to her door, Mrs Althorn said, "Tank you darling, now run home straight, you mada would be looking for you."

When I came home, I just felt that this evening was different. I walked up to the house and as I did the front door flung open; my mum waiting for me. She had had enough. She asked me where I'd been. I explained that I helped Mrs Althorn home with her shopping.

She said, " Yu sure a nat dat bway u de a luk pan, an a lye to me?" (Are you sure it wasn't that boy you went to see and are lying to me?)

I said, "No ma." She grabbed hold of me. I managed to slip from her hand but I was wearing a sleeveless jumper, so she was able to catch hold of it.

She was really in a bad mood tonight. I escaped out of the jumper, leaving it in her hand and ran; I just ran and ran and ran. At this point, I was now aware that my father was on his way home from work. I knew I was in for it tonight. When my mum told my dad, I would surely get a beating.

Then I thought, it is Wednesday night, prayer meeting night and they would be going to someone else's house. I thought to myself, I would lay low until they went to prayer meeting, then go home and do some things that would please them. When they came home from prayer meeting, they wouldn't beat me.

But where could I go till then? And I was hungry. I decided to go around to one of my friend's houses.

Now, they knew that my parent's would not allow me out especially on a week night, so I had to find a reason why I am there that would give me time till the coast was clear.

Last time something like this happened, my friend's mum frogmarched me back home. It happened, as I arrived at their house, that they were going to take the little ones to the park and asked me to join them. I thought this would give me a good chance, then I could slip away and no one will know the difference. I did not know that this day was when my whole life would be turned upside down forever.

CHAPTER 4

Abuse at 'The Park'

We got to Kingsway Park, not far from my friend's house with all the children. At the park I was so surprised to see so many people I knew from school, church and other schools all playing football, rounders or just hanging around. This was new to me as I thought all children went home after school to do chores and stay in until morning.

Two boys that I knew from church came over to me, "What are you doing here?" They asked, "Does your mum and dad know you are here?" I replied, "Yes they do actually!" They spoke to me for a while when I was amongst my friends and the ones I came with.

Another boy came over to us and started chasing us, scattering us. He grabbed hold of my hand and started running, pulling me around the park. I was trying to lose his hold without falling and called for help. I lost my balance and fell straight on my face. I was crying by this point.

By the time I got myself together to get up, a crowd had gathered around me. I suddenly felt they were not there to help me as they were laughing. I was crying and bruised. I tried getting up quickly; as I got up, I started to run.

I just want to get out of there. As I was running, I turned around and a group of boys were following me. They caught up with me and got me to the ground. I began to scream. Someone put a 'cloth-like' thing in my mouth to stop me from screaming. I struggled, I was petrified.

A man with a dog passed by. He shouted, "Leave her alone or I'll call the police!" They chased the man away and I felt dead scared.

I think I fainted. I came to realise I was being repeatedly raped by these boys. When I looked up, the whole park was surrounding me, including the so-called friends that I came with just watching. I looked up hoping someone would rescue me.

I began to pray within myself saying, "God deliver me, don't let them kill me." Just then I heard someone ask, "Who is that?"

When someone told him it was me, I heard the shock in his voice and he replied, "Who? What? Pastor Campbell's daughter?" Then I heard, "No! Do you know who that is? My God!" I heard a shuffle and chasing, and then I was left alone.

He took the cloth out of my mouth as my hands were tied. I just wanted to die. Then I realised that it was Mrs Althorn's son; the one my mum thought I went to see. He pulled me off the ground. I had a skirt on, it was filthy. I couldn't find my underwear.

He wanted to take me home but by this time my parents would be at home, and there was no way I could sneak in without them finding out.

He said he would just have to take me to his mum's; she would know what to do.

He took me to his mother, and we told her everything that had happened. She was so concerned for me, she phoned my parents to let them know where I was. We waited for my parents to come but I fell asleep and woke up the next day in the same position on the couch.

No one came to get me.

The family was moving that morning to Northampton. Not knowing what to do with me, I was sent to school. I arrived at the school gate very frightened and did not know whether to go in or run away but I thought, if I run away where will I go?

Morning break had just ended and I saw school children lining up to go back into school. I thought, I will go in, join the end of the queue and no one will notice me.

As I entered the gate I heard the voice of one of the teachers say, "Nordine Campbell, your dad is in the office looking for you." With that, I turned and ran out at the thought that my dad was at the school.

The rugby teacher chased me down the main road and swooped me up with one arm; he turned around and carried me back to the school kicking and screaming. When we were safely in the school he began to calm me down, and took me to the heads office. My mum was sitting there crying. When she saw me, she began to sob profusely, and my Father wasn't there.

I was asked to sit down and tell them what had happened to me. I began to say that nothing had happened to me, I was so ashamed. Then they began to bring witnesses to testify in detail (they had already questioned the witnesses before I arrived). I just wanted to die, it was so surreal. In my head I was so scared of what my dad was going to say.

The head had called the police; the statement was taken from the witnesses. My mother was asked to take me to the police station later on that day where I was questioned.

My mother had to take me to the hospital to have tests done and then back to the police station for more questioning. We did not get home until about 2am the next morning.

The fear that overcame me was indescribable. How do I face

my dad? My siblings? Where will I sleep? Question after question flashed across my mind like a mighty rushing wind.

As we walked into the house, my father did not look at me. He asked my mum, "Where is my dinner?" My mother was so upset and answered, "You should be asking how your daughter is?" He replied, "My daughters are in them bed."

My mother turned to me and said, "Go and have a bath and then go to bed." My father exclaimed, "Where she going to sleep? Not with my children." Mother replied, "So where do you expect her to sleep?"

With that, my father went outside into the garden and retrieved a garden lounger that was dirty from the children playing on it and said, "She can sleep on that, I don't want my children catching diseases from her." He took the lounger upstairs to the bedroom I shared with my sisters.

After I bathed, I went upstairs and there was the lounger at the bottom of the bed I shared with my sister. He did not speak to me but said to my sister, "I don't want this gal in your bed and if I come up here and see her in the bed I will beat you, you hear?"

In response she said 'Yes Dad." During the night my sister Irene felt sorry for me and told me to come into bed with her but I refused. It was a good thing I didn't; he did come back and checked to see if I was sleeping on the lounger (as he knew that my sister and I were close), but I didn't, I slept on the floor.

I never returned to school again. In those days school leaving age was fifteen. As I was nearing 15, I was not able to finish school.

The confrontation
Parents of the boys insisted on having meetings with my father, asking him not to press charges against the boys. These meetings seemed to go on for ages, every day there would be a meeting. Then my nightmare came when they decided to bring the boys to my house to say sorry to me.

I was so scared I was going to face these boys. I wondered why my dad agreed to this. I felt like it was my fault and nobody believed me.

I was called into the front room. My Father was there along with three other adults in the room. I was told that the boys would come in and apologise to me, then my father will go down to the police station and drop the charges against the boys.

I was angry and felt so ashamed but at the same time intimidated. I was asked to sit down. The boys came in one by one and said, "I am sorry." I was too angry and ashamed to lift my head.

That evening we had a visit from the station sergeant, who came to tell my father that he could not drop the charges because the report had already being filed at the head office and there is nothing they could do about it. Imagine my relief. I started crying, (I just think the Sergeant said that in the hope that my father did not know the law).

In fact, I thought my father was quietly relieved also, as it gave him a reason to tell those people who were pressurising him to drop the charges against those boys.

CHAPTER 5

Homeless

The boys were sentenced to 6 years for the rape and spent time in young offenders' unit.

That may seem like a victory but my life took another turn in my household. I don't think my father forgave me for what had happened to me.

He would not accept food from me. My mother would send me with a cup of tea to him and he would not take it from me. If I should walk into a room and he was on his own, he would get up and walk out.

Therefore, if my mum asked me to go into the same room as him, I would refuse and that would cause an argument.

There was never any peace in the house as long as I was there. I was not attending school, I was told that I would 'amount' to nothing as I had not done any exams; therefore, I was a dunce, and good for nothing and a shame to my family, or so I was told constantly. My father and I would fight all the time.

I just wanted to leave as I had been told that, "Two bulls can't live in one pen, and this is my pen." The only way I could get out of this house and away from my Dad was to get a job.

I would go out every day to look for a job. My first job was in a hat factory as a machinist sewing hats. The day I started the job I was told that I had to start by sewing bows on hats by hand.

I never did get to use the machines; I ended up walking out of the job after the first week because of the wages and I was sick of the racist jokes.

That same day I got a job in Fine Fare supermarket with better pay. My mum used to visit me there; she was very happy and proud that I got a job in a supermarket. I would avoid my father at all costs.

When I got in I would eat and get ready for bed. He would wake up early for work; I would leave my room when he left the house.

The atmosphere in the house was challenging. I loved my siblings but they were too young to understand what was happening. Irene was always supportive and worried about me all the time. There were times when I would go out to youth club and Irene would let me in when I alerted her that I was home, by the click of the pebbles on the window.

Then we realised that the glass from the slatted window that led into the downstairs toilet and bathroom could be removed.

If we were heard by my parents whose room was on the second floor, as we had to pass their room to go upstairs to the upper landing where our bedrooms were, we would be in serious trouble.

Sometimes they would hear footsteps going upstairs and would ask, "Who is that?" And I would answer, "It's me mum! Just went to the toilet." I would change into my night clothes that had been left in the bathroom.

My father thought I was a bad influence on my siblings and felt that I needed to find somewhere to go. He was always saying that.

Then one day there was an argument between my father and me and he took his belt off and started to hit me. I ran into the bathroom which was very small and I was cornered; there was nowhere to run. He continued to hit me with this belt. I cried so much that I was not frightened anymore.

I thought to myself this is enough, I can't do this no more. I asked him to stop and it was as if this was it for him. He had snapped.

While he was hitting me he was also calling me all sorts of names, telling me he should have left me in Jamaica. He said, "You came to destroy my life, you are a demon, you will be nothing."

All sorts of things were in him. I thought to myself this man is going to kill me if I don't stop him. I decided to take the belt from him, so I started to count the times the belt went up and came down. I decided to grab the belt on the next time down and I couldn't miss, I got it.

I dragged the belt, twisted it around my tiny hand and pulled it which caused him to stumble.

I got the belt from out of his hand and hit him with the belt buckle and said, "This is how it feels!"

I did it twice then jumped over him and ran. I knew I would not be able to stay another night in this house; my mother was in tears and my siblings crying. I went to the bedroom, grabbed my bag and ran through the front door on the second floor.

"Where do I go now?" I asked myself. I felt so alone, I felt all alone before but all of a sudden, this felt so different. I was confused, frightened and regretful.

I sat on a wall at the bottom of Cromwell Hill and sobbed my eyes out thinking, where am I going to sleep tonight? I felt that I should go to a relative but I knew that they would take me back.

I couldn't think of a friend I could go to because of the rape and the gossip that followed. No one talked to me anymore and some parents forbid them from going around with me. Then I remembered one person; I knew her and her family liked me and I was always invited to come to their house.

It was getting late in the evening by now, around 8.30pm. I had no choice just until the morning then I would find somewhere to go, I also had my job at Fine Fare.

I went to my friend's house. Her mum and dad were glad to see me but asked what am was doing out at this time. I explained that I just wanted to spend the night till all calmed down at home. I slept at their house that night. The next morning I got up, got ready and went to work.

While I was at work my mum came into the shop asking me to come back home. I said, "No." I could never live another day in the house with that man." She said, "He will not do anything to you anymore. Come back home. I couldn't sleep last night knowing you was out here by yourself. I didn't think you was at work. I just came to check, please come back." Because of my mum I went against my better judgment and went back to the house after work.

My father did not say a word to me. He was dead silent; the walking out of the room when I entered started again, and it was awful. Everyone was on tenterhooks. I dealt with the situation by keeping out of his way. I would come home from work, go straight to the bedroom and would not leave until the next day to go back to work.

I was so frustrated that I just did not want anyone near me and I would push my siblings away as I was afraid that my dad would accuse me of being a bad influence on them, as he has done in the past. I overheard an argument between my mum and dad and he said to my mum, "I don't know why you bring that girl back into my house."

My parents they never argued in front of us. If and when it happened it would be at night when everyone was in bed.

I had to leave again after my father and I had a massive argument and he told me to get out of his house. I went back to my friend's house as I knew it would not be for long.

I went to Bury Park to enrol in the army but I was too young, I had to be 18, at 16, I needed my parent's permission to enrol as a cadet and I knew that was not going to happen.

I managed to rent a small room; I was still working at Fine Fare and my mum used to come and visit me there and would bring me food, making sure I was alright. She never stayed long as she needed to be home for my siblings.

One evening when I was walking in Bury Park a car stopped. I thought they were lost and seeking direction (which often happened in those days). One said, "Excuse me."

I went over to the car that had three Asian-looking guys (there was not many Asian people in Luton). As I approached the car the backdoor flung open, then from the back of me I was pushed into the car, screaming, shouting and fighting. I was hysterical and someone had his hand over my mouth.

The next thing I knew, I woke up in a place I did not know, in a house, my hands tied and my mouth taped. I wanted to scream but could not. I was by myself. I thought they were going to kill me.

The door opened. I was crying. A young Asian man said, "I loose you no scream". He took the tape off my mouth and I screamed. Holding his hand over my mouth he said, "No shout, no hurt you."

I was petrified with fear; I was so overcome with fear that I could not move. I was wondering where were the others that were in the car?

Am I going to be raped again and what will they do to me? All I could do was pray, "Lord don't let this happen to me again, please Jesus. I am so sorry, forgive me, rescue me." I began to think about my family, my father.

The man had gone from the room. While in deep thought, the door opened again and a blond-haired girl, not much older than me, walked in and asked me if I needed a drink.

I said, "No I just want to go home. Where am I and what am I doing here? Who are you?" She said, "You are not on your own. There are other girls here, no one is going to hurt you, come."

She took me into a room where there were about five girls; I was the only black girl there. They were eating and invited me to join them. I refused. Looking around the room, I saw there were three men, one at the door, one near the front door and one at the other end of the room.

I asked where I was and was told that I was in Letchworth (30 miles from Luton). The girls didn't talk to each other, they were just as frightened and confused as I was. I asked the girl that brought me to the room what was going to happen to us. She said that we would stay here tonight and in the morning they would take us somewhere else.

I thought to myself, no way am I going to be taken any where, I am getting out of here. But the windows were locked so were the front and backdoors.

The guys that were there stood watch all night. You could not ask them anything because they did not speak English. I did not sleep that night.

The next morning, I had already decided that I was going to make a run for it, with the first chance I got. I was going nowhere with no one; I would rather die. I was going to take a chance.

I saw a chance when they were taking us to the car; I just saw the chance and I ran and ran.

I didn't know where I was, I just ran. All I knew was that it was very early in the morning and there was hardly anyone around. I managed to find the station and went back to Luton.

I felt like I was the only one in the whole wide world. I couldn't go to the police as I did not know where I had been and who would believe me anyway?

When I came back to Luton, I was frightened to go out in case I saw those men again, so I left my Job. I just wanted to leave Luton but had nowhere to go.

I had a visit from my friend who was upset, saying she did not want to go back home.

I told her she was better off at home as her parents allowed her to go out and I thought she was lucky to have her family.

I left the room I rented because I did not have a job and could not afford the rent. My friend asked me to come by her place, so I said I would.

I explained to her that I would have to leave town but if I could leave my things there I would come and pick them up once I had settled. Her parents said it would be all right to leave my things there.

I decided to spend the night with her then go the next morning.

My friend's father was not at the house when I arrived; her mother is a nurse and would often work night shifts. During the night we were asleep in her bedroom and the door opened and there was her father. My friend said, "Oh no, don't move, he is drunk. Be quiet, he won't hurt you."

I was paralysed with fear as he sexually abused my friend right next to me.

She grabbed hold of me and her fingernail sank into my skin. She could not scream, she just shrieked. When he finished he just got up and walked out of the room. It was as if he did not know I was there, that's how drunk he was.

After he left she just began to cry uncontrollably saying, "I can't take this anymore." I was crying with her as I felt so helpless. I said, "We need to go to the police." She insisted that I didn't call the police as he would take it out on the other children. Then I said, "I am leaving and you are coming with me."

I had no clue where we were going. All I knew I had to leave Luton. So I decided London would be the best place to go. We boarded a train and went to kings X station.

We walked around the area and we talked about our families until it got late. We had very little money left and we had nowhere to sleep; we started to beg so we could eat.

Then someone told us about Centrepoint where we could get something to eat and a bed for the night. That's where we slept on a mattress on the floor with an itchy blanket, but we were grateful.

The next day we went to see someone I knew who lived in North London.

When we got to North London, we hid our bags of clothes under some bushes across the road on the green. We decided we were going as if we were just in the area and decided to pass by.

When we got to the house we were invited in, fed and watered. I then told the truth as it was getting late and we had nowhere to stay.

We were happy when we were told that we could stay the night and that they would try and help us in the morning.

The next day, one of the boys took us to his cousin who was a social worker. She had two children of school age. She gave us a room to stay in until she could sort something out for us, where we could go etc.

CHAPTER 6

Education

I had no qualifications, I had left my family home, I was homeless and had ended up in London at a social worker's house, picking up and dropping her children to and from school.

There was a glimmer of hope. I was grateful for the fact that I was not on the streets, but that was not enough. I had to prove my father wrong, that I was a good for nothing.

I spoke to the Lady and told her my story. By this time my friend had decided that she wanted to go back home as she found it hard to survive in London, but I did not have a choice.

I was introduced to this project in Hackney called the Harambee Project for young people run by this man who we knew by the name of Brother Herman.

The project was held in a big house with three floors. The ground floor was equipped with sewing machines where young people who were interested in tailoring or machining would be taught.

The middle floor had offices with typewriters, there was a library and Brother Herman's office; this is where those that were interested in admin and office work were trained.

Then, on the top floor, there were rooms where tutors would come to teach English, Maths, reading and other training rooms.

After a tour of the building I was brought to Brother Herman's office. He asked me, "What do you want to be?" I replied 'a lawyer."

He told me I can be anything I wanted. I just had to believe! After an induction period, I was called into the office and was told that a place had been made available for me to train as a barrister's clerk. I would be working with a law firm in the city called St Vill's Chambers.

You can imagine my excitement! My job was to go to the office, pick up clients' files and meet one of the barristers at a magistrate court anywhere in London.

On the first day, I was so nervous but I wanted to do this. I was sent to the magistrate's court in Islington, with the name of the barrister I was to meet and handed over the files. I would assist them is obtaining information that was needed in court from the solicitor.

The other part of the job was to solicit clients for the firm. At that time, a number of black families would come to court without a legal representative.

We would approach the black families and ask if they were represented in court. If not, we would recommend our solicitors and fill out legal aid forms for them. Those forms would then be submitted at the office at Harambee Project.

I enjoyed being at Harambee Project as I had a chance to meet other young people and learn new skills; it is where I learnt to do Maths and polish up on my English.

The project was for one year and things seems to have taken a positive turn. I was happy where I was living. Then one day this all came to an abrupt end.

My friends, the young men who introduced me to the social worker, came round to the house as they usually did, but this time it seemed different.

I was called into a room and was asked if I knew t guy. It was one of the guys who was at the park when the rape took place. My first instinct was to deny it, but then I decided against it.

I was informed that he said that I was dangerous because I sent 6 innocent boys to jail by telling the police they raped me; at that moment my world was shattered. How could I convince them that this was not true?

I asked them where they knew him from. They said that they met him and he said he came from Luton. Naturally, they asked if he knew me, and that's when the revelation came. He reckoned that he had spent 6 months in prison for just being there.

I was told I had to leave, because I did not tell them exactly what had happened and they couldn't trust me. One said, "I don't want you accusing me." I tried to explain but they were having none of it; they had made up their minds could not be changed.

The lady I was living with said she was not willing to put me out on the streets, so I could stay until she found me somewhere safe to go.

I was staying in a hostel in Hackney, where I met this lovely young man who was very good to me. He would always want to look after me, making sure I ate.

He would come to the hostel to take me out. He was a gentle man after about six months of being with him, we decided to move in together.

He was a tailor and he used to sew for a company in Savile Row in the West End.

We lived in Wood Green. He himself had a troubled background; he was brought up in the care system. His foster carer was also a tailor and he went on to get formal training and become a professional tailor himself. He also taught me a few tricks of the trade.

I got pregnant; this was such a joyous time, and we had plans of being parents and providing a good future for our baby.

From the start of the pregnancy, I began to have problems. I was in and out of hospital and within three months I had lost the baby. The hospital did tests and found that my inside was so damaged and I had lots of scar tissues which would make it very difficult for me to have children. They announced to me that I would have difficulties in getting pregnant and keeping it.

This was not good news for us. Things didn't get better for us in fact, they got progressively worse. He was angry at the boys as he believed that they took away the chance of having children and that they killed his child.

One evening when I was at home and he had gone out, I had a phone call to say he was on the Green and would I come and meet him there.

This was about 10pm at night. I went out the Green, just at the top of our road. There he was, sitting on the bench. I knew he was intoxicated with drink and he was talking about why this had happened to us and voicing how he was feeling.

It was getting cold so I persuaded him to come with me; I was taking him home.

We got up and he said he couldn't walk because the ground was melting and he was going to sink.

Eventually, I took him home. He told me he was hungry. I had cooked boiled dumplings, yam and bananas with fish. I shared the food out on the plate but he couldn't eat it as he said the dumplings were melting on the plate and the fish was looking at him. Then he said, "The pots are melting. I can't stay in here, the walls are coming in."

I thought, this guy is crazy. What was he talking about? He found the front door and ran outside.

Now I was really worried about him and I chased after him. He had gone back to the Green and I ended up sitting up with him all night. I found out that he went to hang out with some hippies and took blotting paper. I'd never heard of it except the paper we used to blot ink at school. It was drugs!! Speed. to be precise.

He was hallucinating! Our life changed after he lost his job; he began to go to reggae dance. He used to be a soul music man and just went to clubs.

His friends changed and he began take weed and sell small bits, then it went onto more. We were having house parties ourselves; we would cook and had bottle parties.

Eventually from fighting against drugs, I began to smoke it myself. I began to enjoy that life; money was flowing. There was champagne and shopping and house parties.

Things changed when he began to get arrested for drugs and he was in and out of prison.

The womanising started and the trust we had between us faded. The domestic abuse started when I questioned him about staying out at nights and stories that came to me about his relationships with other women.

When we went out together he would take me home at a certain time telling me that it wasn't good for his woman to be out so late.

I thought it never bothered him as before everyone knew us as a couple and we were inseparable.

He would often remind me that I was barren and not able to give him children.

One day, the house where we were living in Finsbury Park, got raided early in the morning.

We were taken to the police station for questioning, then to court. We were remanded in custody and I went into Holloway prison and he went to Pentonville.

We spent a week until we went back to court. It was so challenging; the atmosphere, the chores, and the smell. I spent a lot of time in tears, looking back on my life and considering where I had ended up.

My lawyer came, said I needed someone to stand bail for me at court, and asked if my parents would.

Imagine how I felt when he suggested my parents. I had not seen them for a long time.

I had a feeling that they knew I was ok as my sister Irene surprised me with a visit one day while I was living in Finsbury Park.

I had no choice but to ask. My father agreed to come to the courts to stand bail for me. I was convinced that there is no way he would turn up, but on the day of the court he was there, not happy mind, but he was there! I was put on bail and was bailed to go back to Luton until my court date. My dad was not happy that he had to go to the court, let alone swear on the Bible to tell the truth and nothing but the truth.

He said, "Since me come into this country, me never entered a courtroom and them make me swear on the Bible."

I went back to Luton until the court case. This was the time I said sorry to my father for giving him so much stress.

The morning I was leaving to go to court in London, my brother Gilbert stood by the door and said, "When I am 16, I am coming to live with you." (And he did.)

I stayed in London with friends. My man was kept in prison on remand, then sentenced.

I decided I wanted a new life after my boyfriend told me some other girl was pregnant by him and, that as I could not have children, we should part. I was devastated because I spent so much time supporting him, and now I was of no use to him.

I had to find a new life for myself. I decided to go and study and make my father proud of me. I move to Bethnal Green. My first job was in a mother and toddler group working part-time and I was required to attend a PPA (Pre-School Playgroup Association) course.

The course ran over two years, then I applied for a job in Lambeth as a nursery nurse in a day nursery. For some time I had been suffering with my stomach, each month would be a painful experience and as I got older it got worse. I was diagnosed with fibroids.

Something had to be done. The hospital consultant said that I should go home and get my house in order.

I had one month to prepare for an operation as I might be in for some time. He explained that there might be a chance I would lose my womb due to the damaged tissues and the fibroids.

The thought of losing my womb was so final. I thought there must be another way. I couldn't lose my womb, I was still young. I decided to go for a second opinion. I went to see a private doctor took tests. They said there was nothing they could do for me

My friend took me to a palm reader, no joy there either. I went to see someone who would give me a bath while I was there waiting to see this woman. The other women was talking of how good this person was and sharing stories but when I went into the room to see her my head felt like it was swelling and my heart started to beat faster.

She began to share things she could see in my life, in my past and future. She said she would give me a bath and I would be healed and all the spells that had been spoken over me would be broken. Then she gave me a towel and sent me to the bathroom to change before she came in to give me a bath.

When I left her room I had a desperate urge to leave. I dropped what she gave me and ran out. I just couldn't get out fast enough.

I went everywhere trying to find answers and a reversal of the inevitable, Yes; I went to church, I even went to the Hare Krishna temple to seek inner peace, I prayed all the prayers and chanted all the mantras but the day of my appointment arrived.

My mother came to London to be with me.

While in the hospital I was visited by a young lady about 16 years old; she was the daughter of the hospital chaplain.

She came to my bedside and introduced herself. Next to my bed there was a copy of the Bhagavadgita from the Krishna temple. She asked me what it was. I explained to her what it was and where I got it from.

She began to minister to me that Jesus was the only and true God and that if I accepted Jesus as my saviour, he would heal me. I told her I knew about Jesus because my father was a preacher man; knowing full well that I had given up completely.

She offered to pray with me and asked God to open my mind to him and to give me the faith to believe in him.

The next morning was my operation day. As they were about to take me to the theatre, the young lady came again and offered to pray with me before I went down to the theatre.

This time her prayer was very intense. She believed that God would give me a sign of who he was and my faith would be restored. She had tears in her eyes.

On the way to the theatre, I thought about the prayers and how serious she was; the thought came to me that this might be the last chance I had to find God even at this final moment, before I went under the knife.

When I was in the room where the nurse gave me my final preparation before going into the theatre I said, "Ok, if you are God then you have to prove yourself to me because right now, I am confused."

The next thing I knew I was in the ward all bandaged up and in the worse pain I have ever experienced and I have had other operations over the years.

The nurse came into the room and said, "Good to see you are awake. "Did you know that you are a miracle?" I did not understand what she was saying so I did not respond. She said, "The doctors will be around to check on you soon," and she gave something for my pain.

I don't know how long it was but I awoke with a nurse standing over me. She said, "I came to see this miracle lady." I said, "That's the second time I heard that today." She then said, "Has nobody told you what happened?" I said, "No. What?"

My mum was at my bedside. She said, "You had complications during your operation. What should take 1 hour took almost 6 hours. You bled so much that you went into cardiac arrest, there was nothing they could do for you.

The surgeon pronounced you gone and instructed the nurses to prepare you and they will have to inform your mother.

When the nurses were preparing you, you began to breathe on your own. The surgeon was amazed. When they checked, you were still alive but unfortunately they could not save your womb, but you are alive." She was so excited, my mum was crying.

I was happy to be alive but I was so disappointed that I had to lose my womb.

That might sound selfish but I was so confused because on one hand I had victory but on the other hand I lost my chance of ever having children and I was only 25 years old. A sacrifice was made for life. I was crying but my tears were twofold.

The surgeon came to see me and told me the story and that my insides were very scary to operate on due to the rape, and then I developed fibroids that grew like a bunch of grapes and attached themselves to my scared tissues, which made it difficult to cut away.

During the operation, I started to bleed so they had to make a life-threatening decision to take my womb in order to spare my life. He assured me that I would heal and live a life free from pain.

The young lady came to see me and she was overwhelmed with the news and was thanking God on my behalf. She began to tell me what God had done for me, how he made the impossible possible, and how much he loved me so much. She asked if I was ready to accept Jesus as Lord over my life and I accepted Jesus in my life on my hospital bed.

I asked God why this had happened to me. I received this scripture in: **Isaiah chapter 54: 1-4.**
Sing, O barren, thou that didst not bear; break forth into singing, and cry aloud, thou that didst not travail with child: for more are the children of the desolate than the children of the married wife, saith the LORD.

[2] *Enlarge the place of thy tent, and let them stretch forth the curtains of thine habitations: spare not, lengthen thy cords, and strengthen thy stakes;*

³ For thou shalt break forth on the right hand and on the left; and thy seed shall inherit the Gentiles, and make the desolate cities to be inhabited.

⁴ Fear not; for thou shalt not be ashamed: neither be thou confounded; for thou shalt not be put to shame: for thou shalt forget the shame of thy youth, and shalt not remember the reproach of thy widowhood any more.

CHAPTER 7

Reconciliation

I took two months sick leave from my job as a supervisor in a day nursery in Lambeth. I decided I was not going to go back to that job and applied for a job in Camden as a officer in charge of a 60 place day nursery in Camden and I got the Job!!!

I loved my new job. However, my challenges came through racism within the council staff, especially in management. I was the first black senior manager ever employed at that level, even though most of their workforce such as nursery nurses, cleaners and cooks were black people, but they felt I was above my station.

There was a line manager by the name of Brian Haddow who felt that the department needed a bit of colour and he was impressed at the interview and decided to give me a chance.

I am so grateful to him. They sent me to Caversham Day Nursery because it was not thriving and it was on the verge of closing down. With the help of God and some wonderful staff, I was able to turn the place around.

One afternoon, I invited my parents to come and see what I was doing. I invited them to come and have lunch with me. We were privileged to have this wonderful cook that I persuaded to come over to our nursery to work; the children and visitors experienced a new delight in English and Caribbean cuisine.

My parents accepted my invitation and the kitchen staff laid on a feast in the staffroom with table linen on their arrival. They were welcomed, shown around the nursery and were introduced to the children. I had things to attend to as it was a working day, but the staff took care of my family and I joined them later in the staffroom.

I greeted them and sat down and as I sat down my mum nudged my dad and said, "Say to her what you said to us." Then my dad said, "I am glad you invited us to come and we was fed and watered.

I can see that you are really loved. I just want to say I am so proud of you and to see what you have achieved and, I love you."

Can you imagine the rush I felt? Never in my wildest dreams could I have ever imagined I would hear what I was hearing.

There was not a dry eye in the place. He came and hugged me for the first time I could remember. After that experience I had such a surge of confidence, I felt that I could move mountains.

I enrolled at North London University in Holloway Road, to do a part-time 2-year Diploma in Social Science with the support of my friend Paul who encouraged me to go for it. Even through my emotional pain, I did an Open University Professional certificate in Management.

My life began to excel. I bought the flat I was living in, in Bethnal Green and I bought a car; I was debt free.

I was approached by the children and families' department in Camden and asked if I would consider fostering young pregnant girls. I was delighted and started the assessment.

One evening whilst I was at University, I received a phone call from my brother Glen. He said, "Nords. I've found Jesus." I replied, "Are you sure? You have to be careful, make sure you have found the right Jesus." He was so happy, he said, "I know it's the right Jesus and I want you to come with me and see."

(I was not attending a church.) He came to meet me that night after lessons, took me to Wembley to this flat where there were young people doing bible studies; they were on fire for the Lord.

My brother left me in a room with one such youth and the young man was ministering to me from the Bible and every scripture he had read.

He was telling me my story. At one point I thought that my brother had told him things about me and I started to get a bit upset.

Then I thought, he doesn't know some of the things this young man was telling me. It was powerful, I never heard the Gospel preached like that before (they were into end time Prophesy).

A few days later, they wanted to come to my flat to pray and I agreed. Mission to London came to Earls Court; I was blown away to see people pray in the streets and in the tube. I was part of that awesome move of God.

I began to foster a young woman who was pregnant. I had the privilege to be her birth partner to a lovely son. One Friday evening getting ready to leave work, I received a phone call. My brother Glen asked me to wait for him as he was coming to meet me as God has answered my prayers.

When he arrived, he came with a beautiful 2 year old. He asked me if I would keep her for the weekend as her mum left her with him and he needed to go and find her. After finding her mother who had so many challenges in her life,

I took her and her children under my wings 20 years later, we are still in touch.

Over the years, I fostered over 100 children. I support children in Kenya, Uganda, and Jamaica and have adopted three children in Ghana.

They are all married with children and they have given me 5 grandchildren.

My daughter Martha is a business teacher. She is married with 2 children, Nordine and Chris.

Maxwell is an ordained minister, businessman and Pastor for the Centre of Hope Global Ministries in Ghana. He is married with two boys.

Vincent is an author, musician and interpreter. He is married with 2 children, Lord Campbell and Nordine.

I thank God for His mercies and His grace.

I bought my second flat in Dalston near the famous Ridley Road Market.

My father and mother became regular visitors to the market and often came to stay with me. Our relationship was fully restored.

My father went home to be with the Lord on 23rd August 1996 after a massive stroke in Luton. R.I.P. Daddy.

I went back to Luton again in 1996, this time to help Pastor the church with my mother and my sister Hildia.

Many are the afflictions of the righteous,
But the L*ord* *delivers him out of them all.*
Psalm 34:19

In God we trust.

Journey to Purpose notes

JOURNEY TO PURPOSE – MY LIFE OF PURPOSE

JOURNEY TO PURPOSE – MY LIFE OF PURPOSE

JOURNEY TO PURPOSE – MY LIFE OF PURPOSE

JOURNEY TO PURPOSE – MY LIFE OF PURPOSE

JOURNEY TO PURPOSE – MY LIFE OF PURPOSE

JOURNEY TO PURPOSE – MY LIFE OF PURPOSE

JOURNEY TO PURPOSE – MY LIFE OF PURPOSE

JOURNEY TO PURPOSE – MY LIFE OF PURPOSE

JOURNEY TO PURPOSE – MY LIFE OF PURPOSE

JOURNEY TO PURPOSE – MY LIFE OF PURPOSE

JOURNEY TO PURPOSE – MY LIFE OF PURPOSE

JOURNEY TO PURPOSE – MY LIFE OF PURPOSE

JOURNEY TO PURPOSE – MY LIFE OF PURPOSE

JOURNEY TO PURPOSE – MY LIFE OF PURPOSE

JOURNEY TO PURPOSE – MY LIFE OF PURPOSE

JOURNEY TO PURPOSE – MY LIFE OF PURPOSE

JOURNEY TO PURPOSE – MY LIFE OF PURPOSE

JOURNEY TO PURPOSE – MY LIFE OF PURPOSE

JOURNEY TO PURPOSE – MY LIFE OF PURPOSE

JOURNEY TO PURPOSE – MY LIFE OF PURPOSE

JOURNEY TO PURPOSE – MY LIFE OF PURPOSE

JOURNEY TO PURPOSE – MY LIFE OF PURPOSE

JOURNEY TO PURPOSE – MY LIFE OF PURPOSE

www.ingramcontent.com/pod-product-compliance
Lightning Source LLC
Chambersburg PA
CBHW020658300426
44112CB00007B/440